THIS BOOK BELONGS TO

____

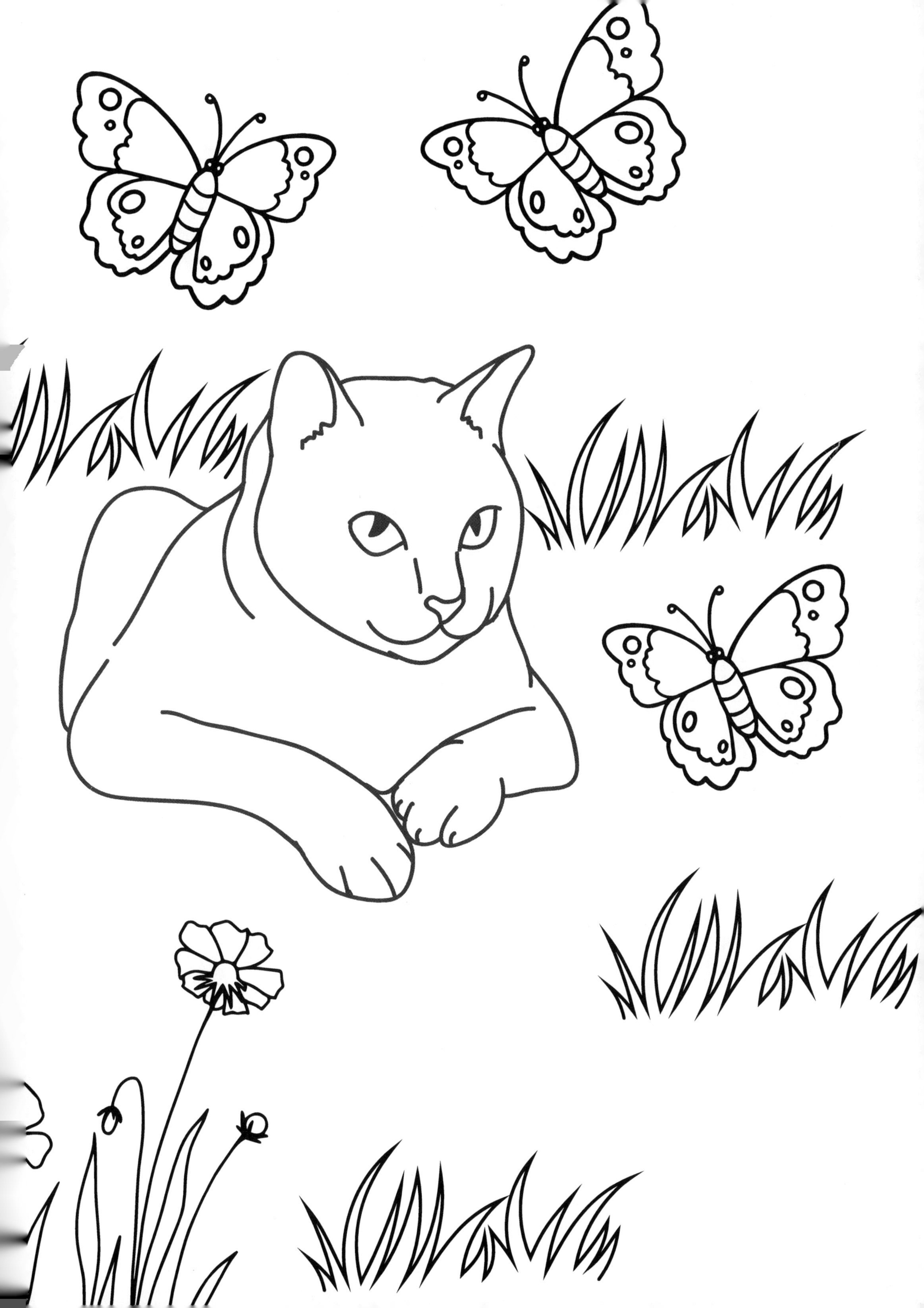

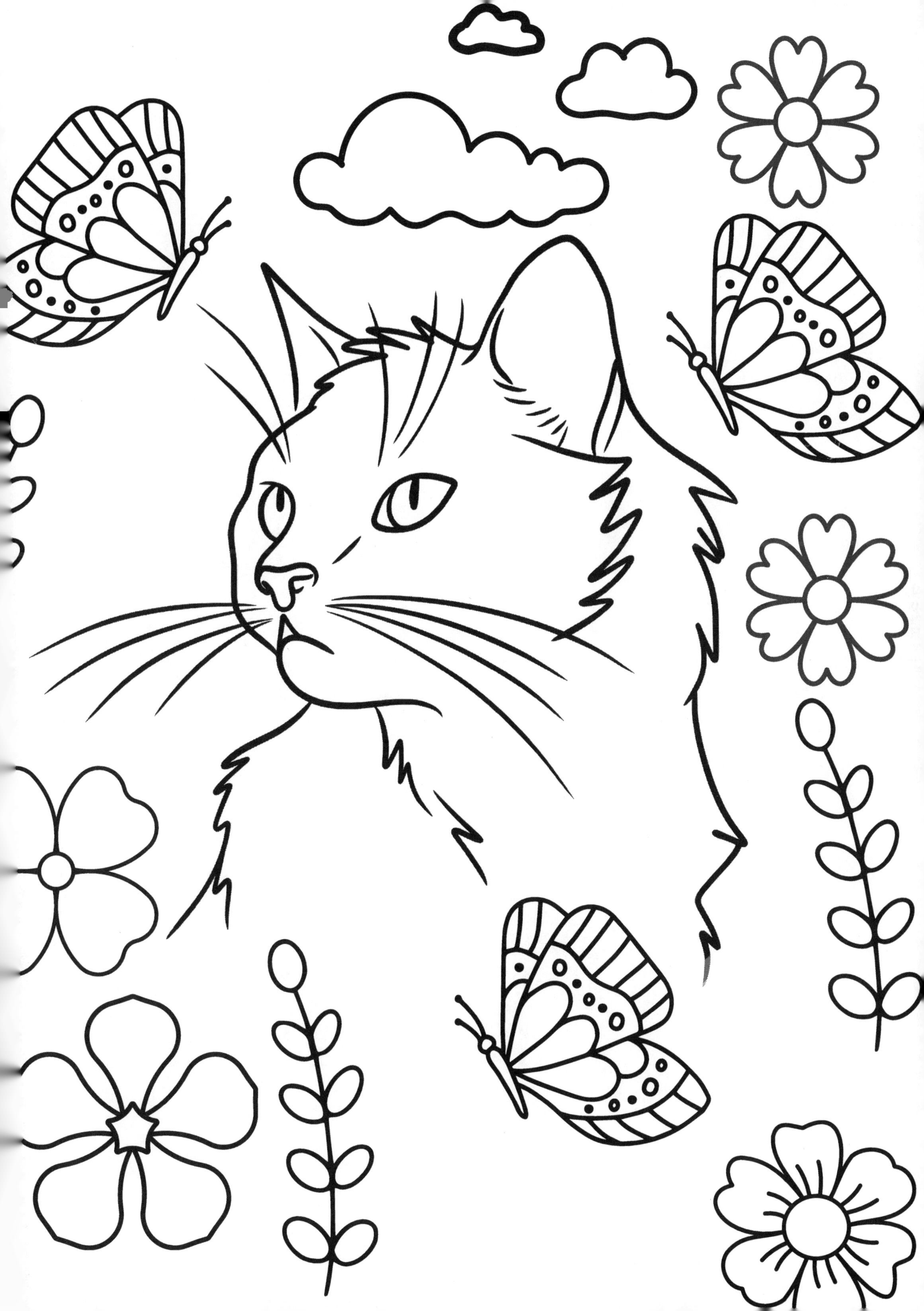

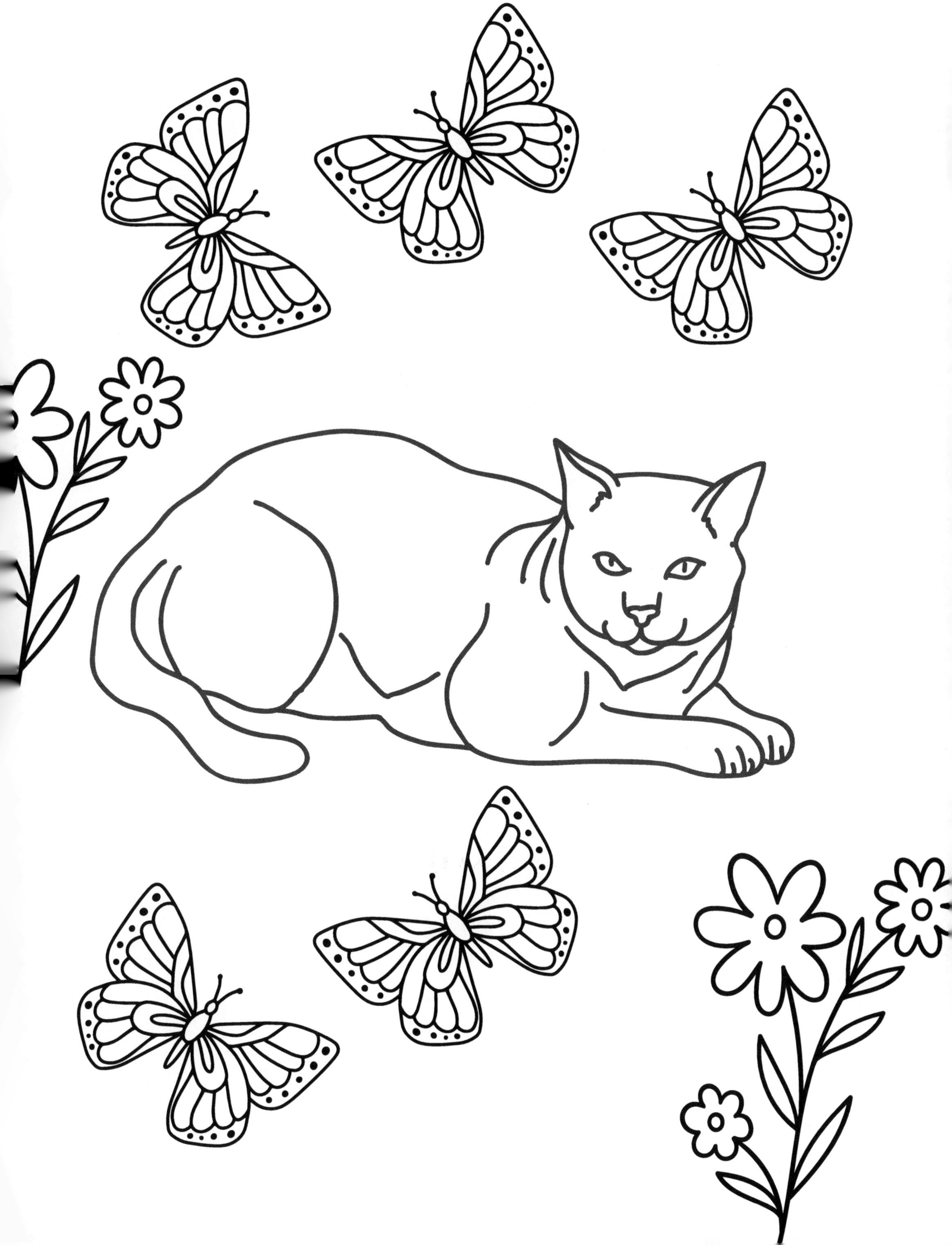

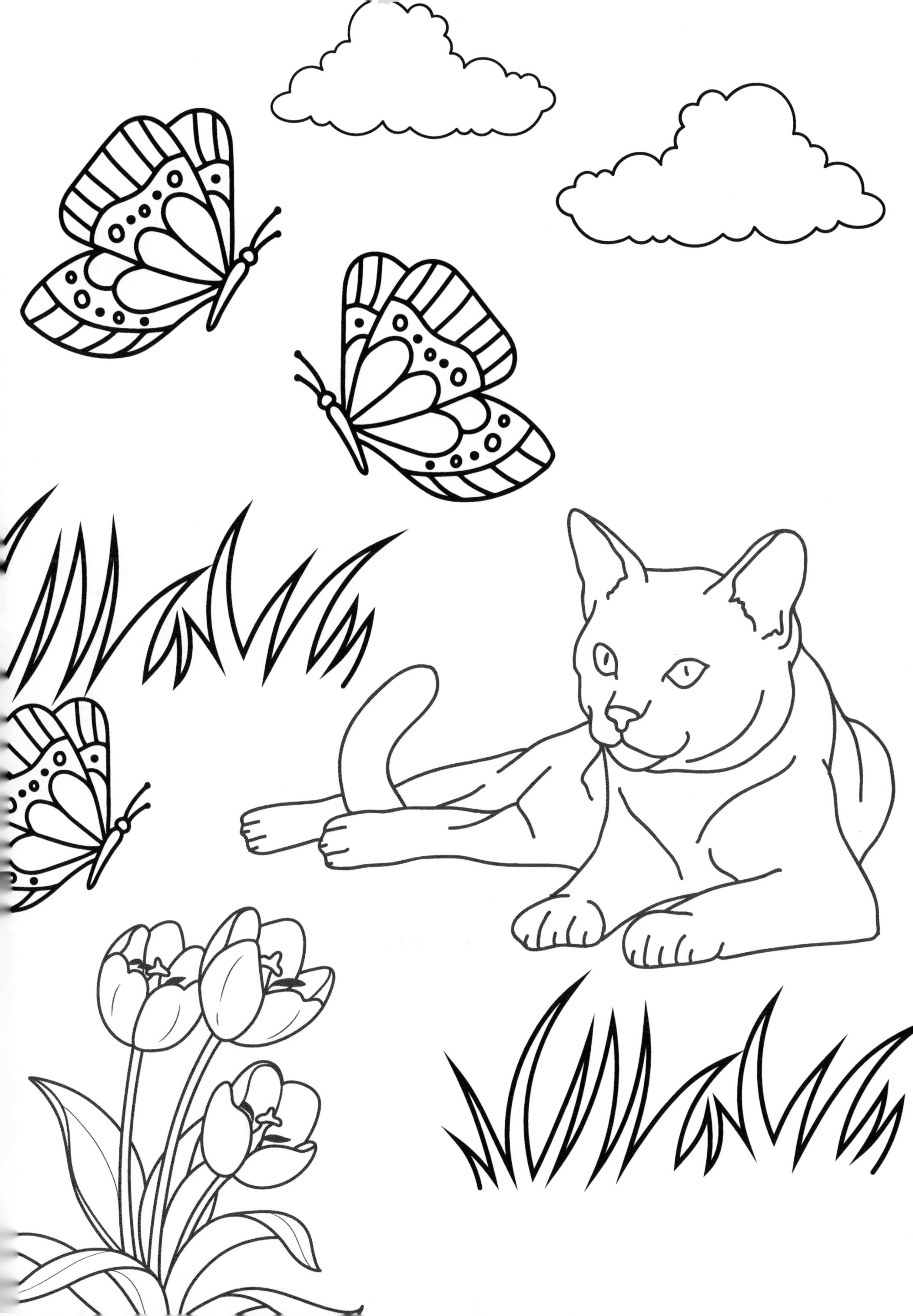

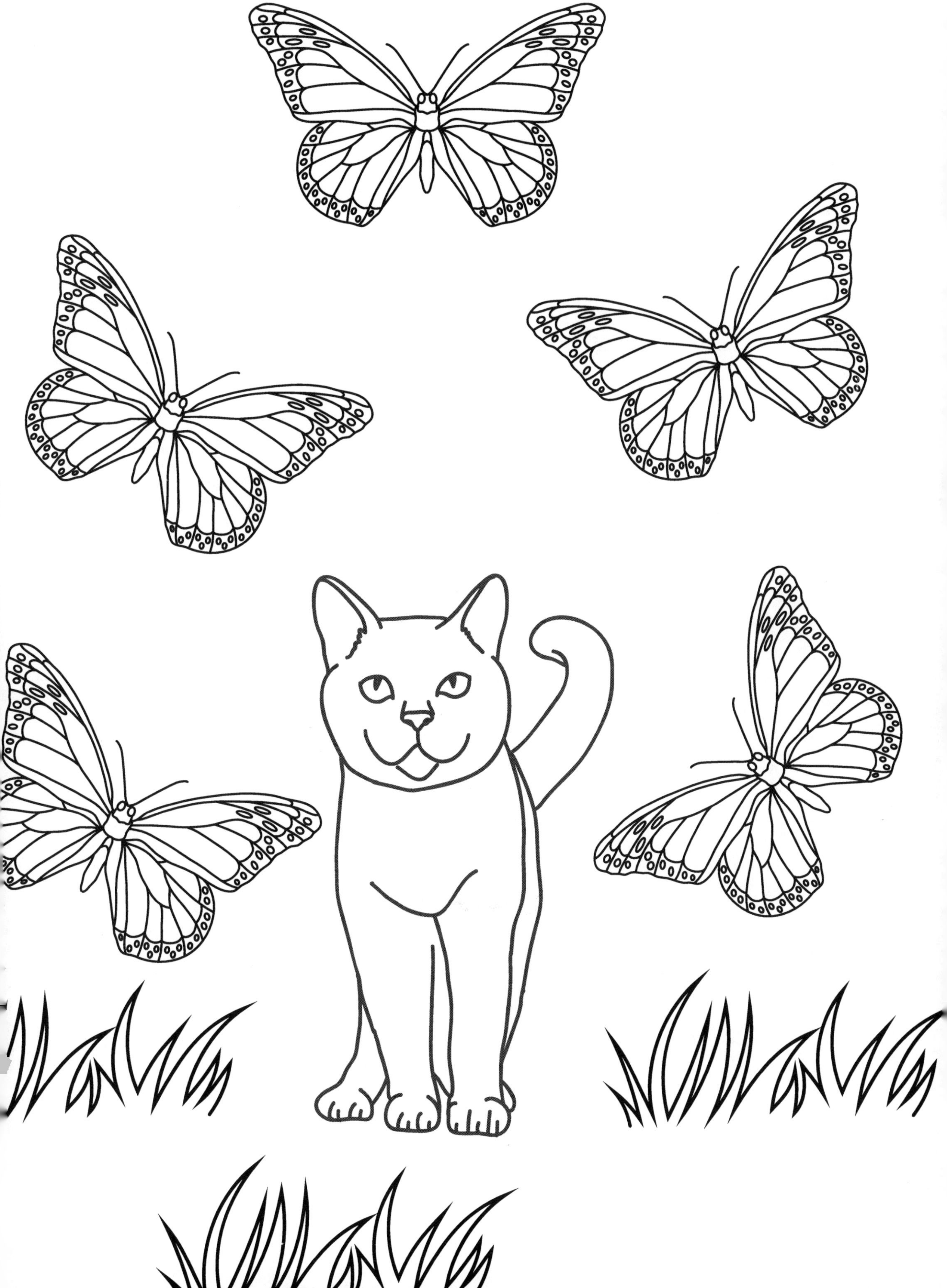

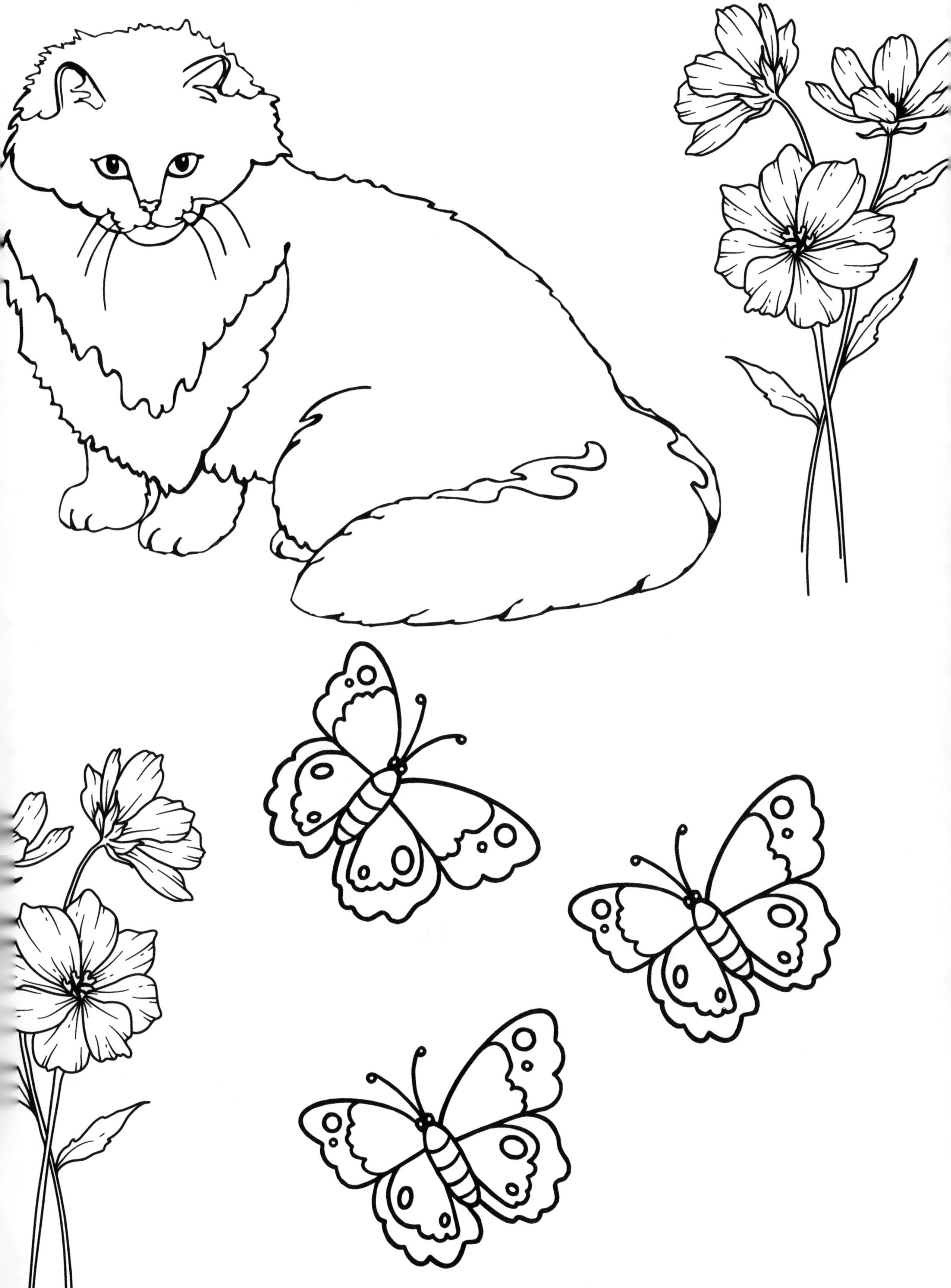

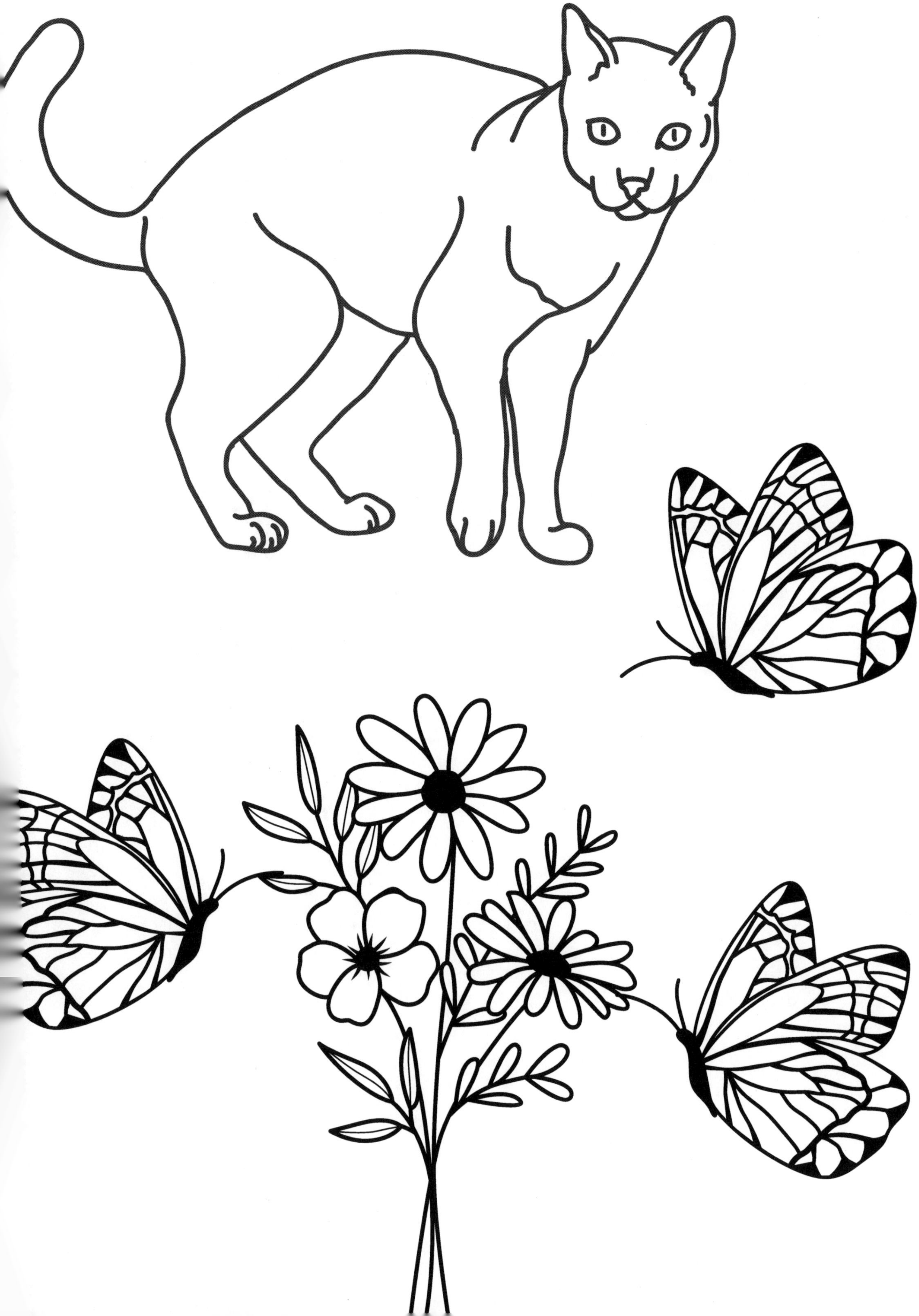

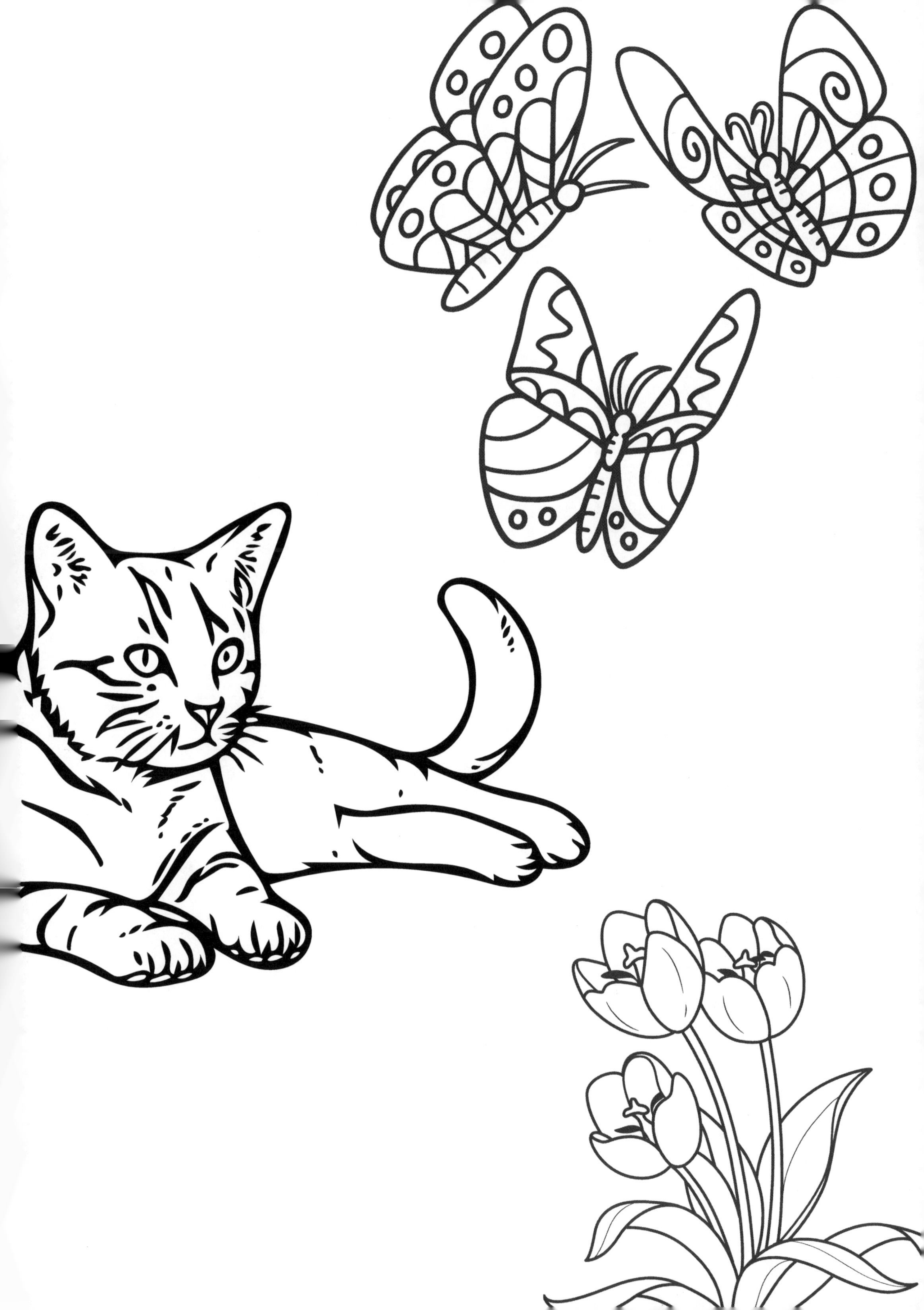

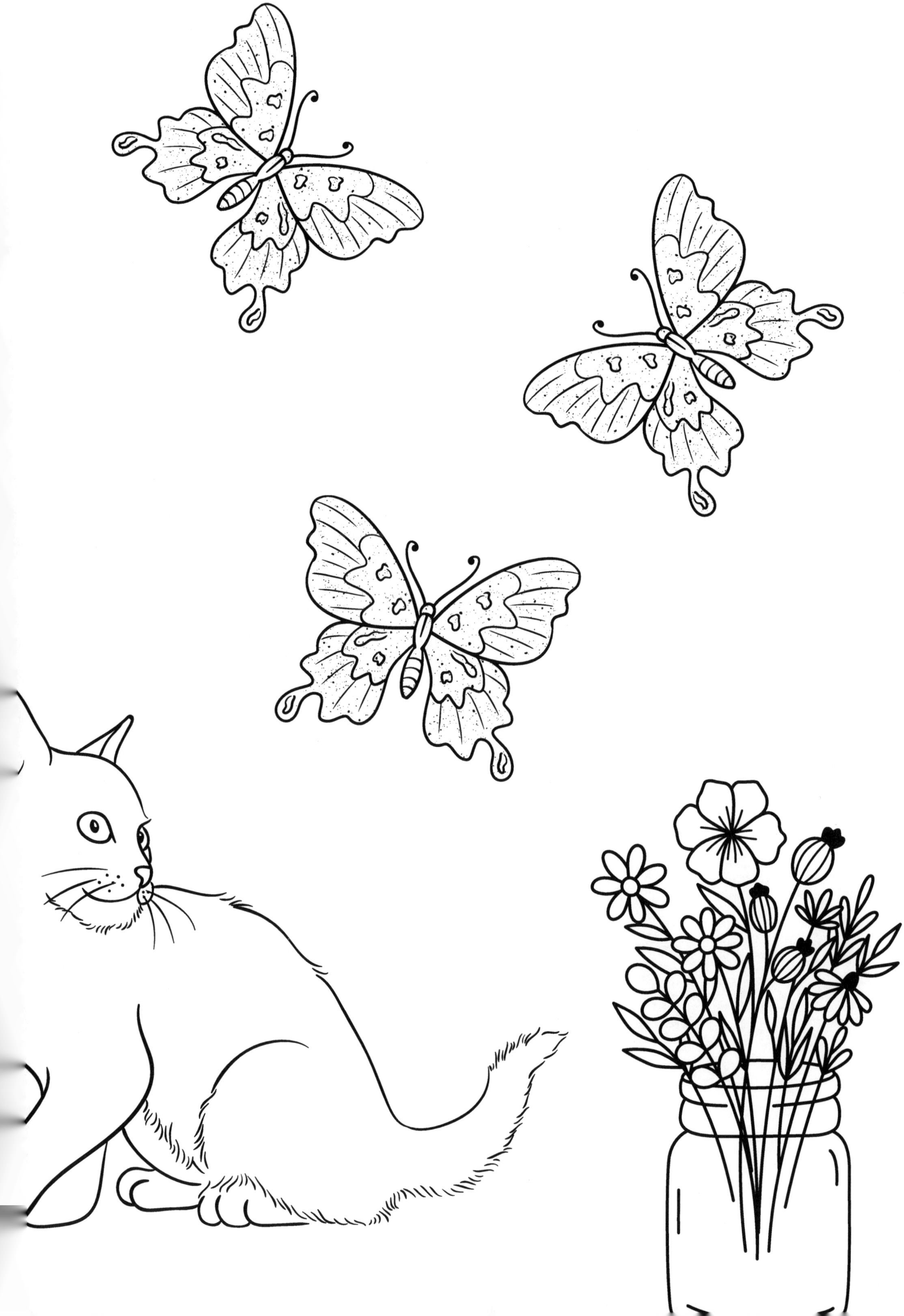

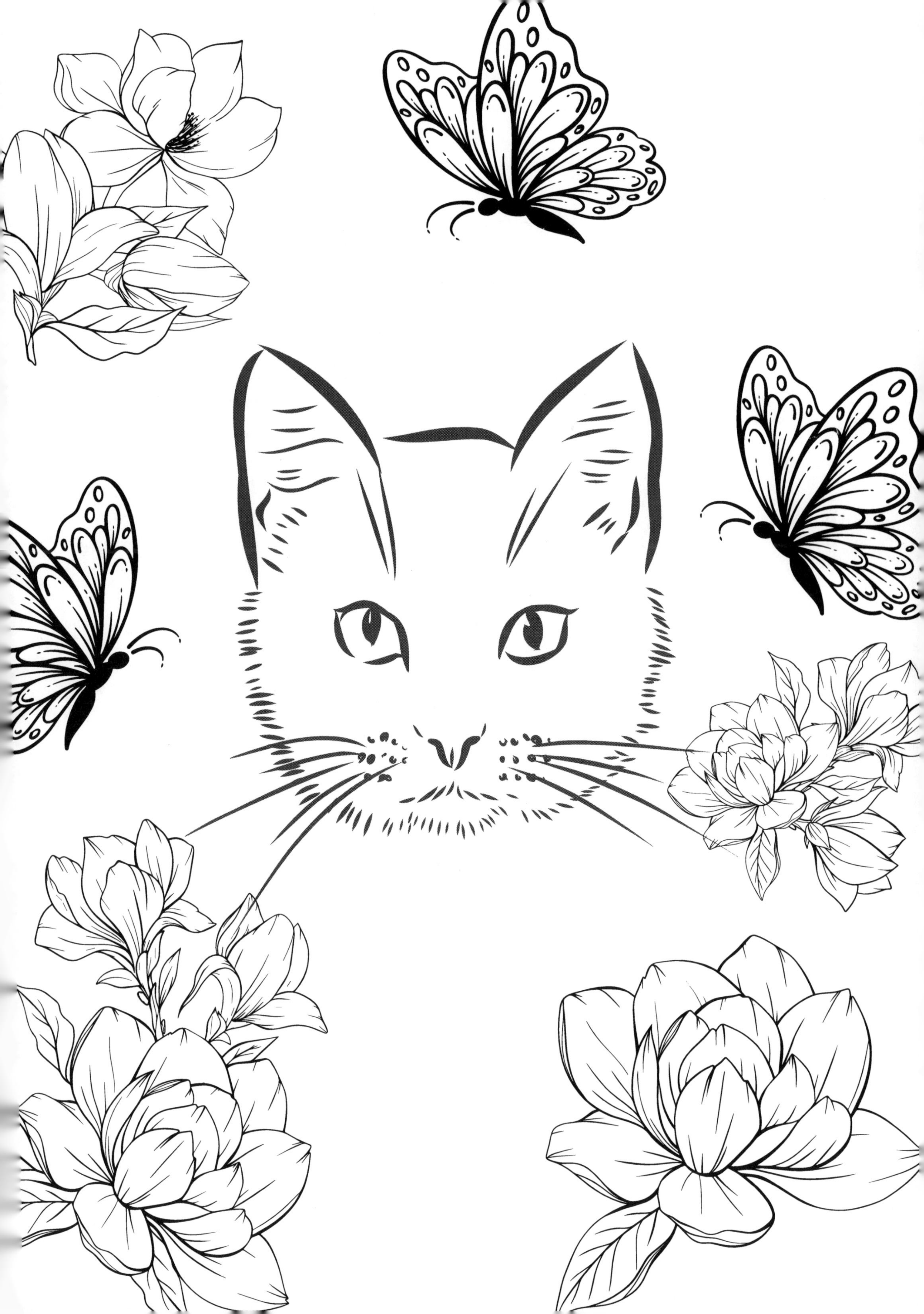

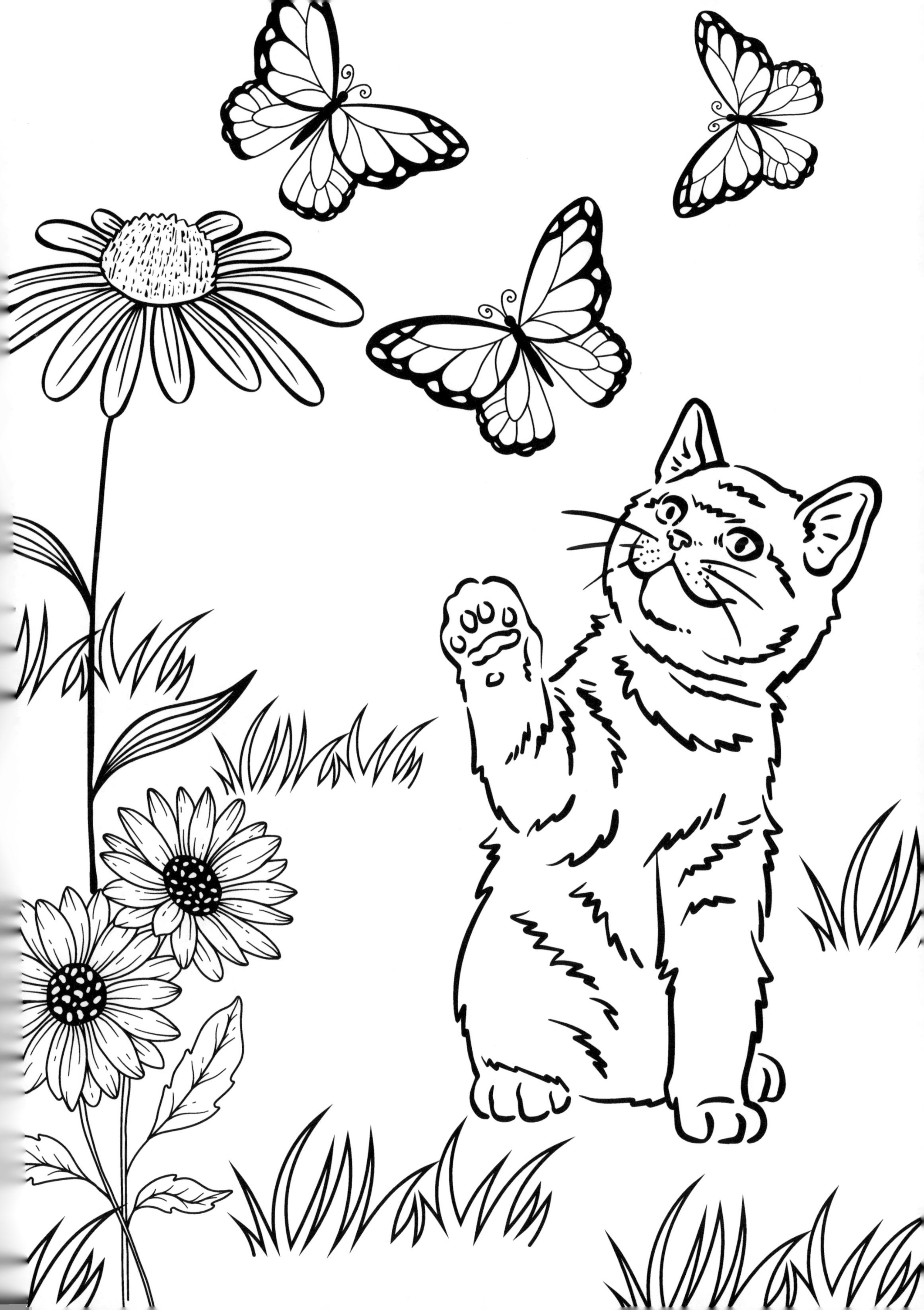

Made in United States
Orlando, FL
18 December 2024

56002634R00015